My Daily Cup of Energizer

Finding Strength, Joy, and Purpose Each Day through HIS Word'

Gerard Assey

My Daily Cup of Energizer:
Finding Strength, Joy, and Purpose Each Day through HIS Word'

By
Gerard Assey

Published by:
Gerard Assey
19/18, Palli Arasan Street
Anna Nagar East
Chennai - 600 102

ISBN: 978-81-971121-2-6

(Image from Freepik.com at 'https://www.Freepik.com' Thank You)

Table of Contents

Introduction

Welcome to '**My Daily Cup of Energizer:** ***Finding Strength, Joy, and Purpose Each Day through HIS Word'*** a sanctuary of solace and strength, crafted to infuse your mornings with hope and vigor. In the hustle and bustle of life, amid the myriad of responsibilities and uncertainties, this book stands as a beacon of light, guiding you towards a day filled with positivity and inspiration.

Picture this: as you wake up each morning, the aroma of freshly brewed coffee fills the air, mingling with the gentle rustle of pages as you open this book. With each sip of your favorite brew, may you also drink deeply from the wellspring of wisdom found within these pages.

In a world often fraught with challenges and trials, 'My Daily Cup of Energizer' seeks to be a steadfast companion, offering you daily doses of encouragement and upliftment. Through the timeless truths found in the pages of the Bible and the exemplary life of Jesus Christ, you'll embark on a journey of discovery, finding practical insights to navigate life's twists and turns with unwavering faith and resilience.

This book is not merely a collection of words; it's a lifeline, a source of strength to lean on when the burdens of life weigh heavy on your shoulders. It's a reminder that you are not alone, that there is a higher power at work, guiding your steps and showering you with love and grace.

As you immerse yourself in the pages of "My Daily Cup of Energizer," may you find renewed energy and courage to face whatever challenges come your way.

May the words penned within these pages serve as a balm to your soul, soothing your worries and igniting a flame of hope within your heart.

So, dear reader, as you embark on this journey, may you embrace each day with renewed vigor and purpose. May you find solace in the promises of God and strength in the example set by Jesus Christ. And may you emerge from the pages of this book, ready to tackle whatever the day may bring, armed with faith, resilience, and an unwavering sense of hope.

Day 1: Daybreak Devotion

Bible Verse: "*The steadfast love of the Lord never ceases; his mercies never come to an end; they are new every morning; great is your faithfulness.*" - Lamentations 3:22-23

Explanation: The verse from Lamentations is a profound reminder of the unceasing love and faithfulness of God. It emphasizes the concept of renewal and fresh beginnings each day, as His mercies are inexhaustible and His faithfulness unwavering. This verse invites us to start each day with a heart filled with gratitude and anticipation for the new mercies God has in store for us.

Biblical Examples: One powerful example from the Old Testament that illustrates the concept of God's mercies and faithfulness is the story of David's repentance and restoration after his affair with Bathsheba (2 Samuel 12). Despite David's grievous sin, when confronted by the prophet Nathan, he repented wholeheartedly. And even though there were consequences for his actions, such as the death of his son, God forgave him and continued to use him as a man after His own heart.

In the New Testament, we see a beautiful example of Jesus' model of forgiveness and grace in His interaction with Peter after Peter's denial. Despite Peter's threefold denial of Jesus, upon His resurrection, Jesus not only forgave Peter but also reinstated him into His service (John 21:15-19). This illustrates God's unfathomable love and faithfulness, which extends even to the most broken and repentant hearts.

Application: As we begin each day, let us reflect on the steadfast love and faithfulness of God, thanking Him for His mercies that are new every morning. Let us also strive to emulate His love and forgiveness in our interactions with others, extending grace and compassion to those who may have wronged us. By starting each day with a heart full of gratitude and forgiveness, we open ourselves to experience the transformative power of God's love in our lives and in the lives of those around us.

Day 2: Strength in Weakness

Bible Verse: *"But he said to me, 'My grace is sufficient for you, for my power is made perfect in weakness.'"* - 2 Corinthians 12:9a

Explanation: In this verse, the apostle Paul recounts his plea to God to remove a thorn in his flesh, to which God responds with the assurance that His grace is sufficient. This verse highlights the paradoxical nature of God's strength being made perfect in our weakness. It teaches us that when we acknowledge our limitations and weaknesses, we open ourselves to receive God's strength and power working through us.

Biblical Examples: In the Old Testament, we find the story of Moses, who initially doubted his ability to lead the Israelites out of bondage in Egypt. Despite his insecurities and feelings of inadequacy, Moses trusted in God's strength and provision. In Exodus 3-4, God reassures Moses of His presence and promises to be with him, demonstrating that His power is made perfect in human weakness.

In the New Testament, Jesus Himself provides the ultimate example of finding strength in weakness during His temptation in the wilderness (Matthew 4:1-11). Faced with the adversary's temptations, Jesus relied on the Word of God to resist temptation, showing us that even in our weakest moments, we can draw strength from the truths found in Scripture.

Application: As we encounter moments of weakness and inadequacy in our lives, let us remember Paul's words and find comfort in the sufficiency of God's grace. Instead of trying to rely solely on our own strength, let us surrender our weaknesses to God, trusting in His power to work through us. By embracing our vulnerabilities and allowing God's strength to shine through, we can experience a newfound sense of empowerment and confidence in facing life's challenges.

Day 3: Courage in the Face of Fear

Bible Verse: *"Be strong and courageous. Do not be afraid or terrified because of them, for the Lord your God goes with you; he will never leave you nor forsake you."* - Deuteronomy 31:6

Explanation: In Deuteronomy 31:6, Moses encourages Joshua and the Israelites to be strong and courageous as they prepare to enter the Promised Land. This verse speaks to the universal human experience of fear and uncertainty but offers reassurance that God's presence and faithfulness will never waver.

Biblical Examples: One powerful example of courage in the face of fear is seen in Joshua's leadership as he succeeded Moses. Joshua was tasked with leading the Israelites into the Promised Land, facing formidable challenges and opposition along the way. Despite the uncertainties and potential dangers, Joshua demonstrated unwavering faith and courage, trusting in God's promises and guidance (Joshua 1).

In the New Testament, we see Jesus as the ultimate model of courage in the face of fear. In Mark 4:35-41, Jesus calms a raging storm while His disciples tremble with fear. He demonstrates His authority over nature, showing His disciples that they need not fear, for He is with them always.

Application: To apply this verse in our lives, we must first acknowledge our fears and uncertainties, recognizing that they are a natural part of the human experience. Then, we can choose to trust in God's presence and promises, knowing that He goes before us and never leaves us alone. Step out in faith, facing challenges with courage and confidence, knowing that God is with you every step of the way.

Day 4: Embracing Forgiveness

Bible Verse: *"Bear with each other and forgive one another if any of you has a grievance against someone. Forgive as the Lord forgave you."* - Colossians 3:13

Explanation: Colossians 3:13 emphasizes the importance of forgiveness in the Christian life. It challenges believers to extend grace and forgiveness to others, just as they have received forgiveness from God. Forgiveness is a transformative act that brings healing and reconciliation, both to the forgiver and the forgiven.

Biblical Examples: A powerful example of forgiveness in the Old Testament is seen in the story of Joseph and his brothers (Genesis 45:1-15). Despite being betrayed and sold into slavery by his own brothers, Joseph chooses to forgive them when they come to him in need during a famine. He recognizes God's hand in his circumstances and extends grace and mercy to his brothers, ultimately leading to reconciliation and restoration of their relationship.

In the New Testament, Jesus exemplifies radical forgiveness on the cross as He prays for forgiveness for those who crucify Him (Luke 23:34). His act of forgiveness demonstrates the depth of God's love and grace, offering redemption and reconciliation to all who repent and believe.

Application: To apply this verse in our lives, we must first recognize the importance of forgiveness in our relationships. Choose to release bitterness and resentment, extending grace and forgiveness to those who have wronged us. Remember that forgiveness is not condoning or excusing the offense but rather releasing the burden of anger and hurt. As we forgive others, we experience the liberating power of God's grace in our own lives and contribute to healing and reconciliation in our relationships.

Day 5: Cultivating Gratitude

Bible Verse: *"Give thanks in all circumstances; for this is God's will for you in Christ Jesus."* - 1 Thessalonians 5:18

Explanation: The verse from 1 Thessalonians 5:18 is a powerful reminder of the importance of cultivating gratitude in our lives. It calls us to give thanks not only in times of abundance and joy but also in the midst of challenges and trials. Gratitude is not just a fleeting emotion but a deliberate choice to acknowledge and appreciate God's blessings, regardless of our circumstances.

Biblical Examples: A striking example of gratitude amidst adversity is found in the story of Paul and Silas in Acts 16:25-34. Despite being beaten and imprisoned for their faith, Paul and Silas choose to sing praises to God in the darkness of their cell. Their act of worship not only demonstrates their unwavering faith but also leads to a miraculous intervention from God, resulting in their freedom and the salvation of their jailer and his household.

In the New Testament, we see Jesus Himself model gratitude before feeding the five thousand (John 6:11). Instead of focusing on the scarcity of resources, Jesus gives thanks for what they have, demonstrating gratitude for God's provision. This act of thanksgiving precedes a miraculous multiplication of food, showcasing the power of gratitude to unlock God's blessings.

Application: To apply this verse in our lives, we must cultivate a habit of daily gratitude. Start by intentionally acknowledging and thanking God for His goodness and provision each day, regardless of the circumstances. Keep a gratitude journal or simply take a few moments each morning or evening to reflect on the blessings in your life. By shifting our focus from what we lack to what we have been given, we open ourselves to experience a deeper sense of joy and contentment in God's abundant grace.

Day 6: Trusting God's Timing

Bible Verse: *"For everything there is a season, and a time for every matter under heaven."* - Ecclesiastes 3:1

Explanation: Ecclesiastes 3:1 reminds us of the sovereignty of God over time and seasons. It speaks to the divine orchestration of events in our lives, each happening according to God's perfect timing. While we may desire immediate answers and outcomes, this verse encourages us to trust in God's wisdom and providence, knowing that He works all things for our good and His glory.

Biblical Examples: A profound example of trusting God's timing is seen in the lives of Abraham and Sarah as they waited for the fulfillment of God's promise of a son (Genesis 21:1-7). Despite their advanced age and years of waiting, God remained faithful to His promise and miraculously provided Isaac in His appointed time. Their story teaches us the importance of patience and perseverance as we wait for God's promises to be fulfilled.

In the New Testament, we see Jesus exemplify patience and trust in God's timing throughout His ministry. On multiple occasions, Jesus deferred to His Father's timing, such as when He waited until the appointed time to reveal Himself as the Messiah (John 2:4; 7:6-8). His life serves as a model of obedience and trust in God's sovereign plan, even when it involved waiting and uncertainty.

Application: To apply this verse in our lives, we must surrender our desires and timelines to God, trusting that His timing is perfect. Embrace patience and perseverance as you wait on the Lord, knowing that He is working behind the scenes for your good. Seek His guidance and direction in prayer, asking for the grace to trust in His timing even when it may not align with our own expectations. By relinquishing control and placing our faith in God's sovereign plan, we can experience a deep sense of peace and assurance in His providential care.

Day 7: Overcoming Anxiety

Bible Verse: *"Do not be anxious about anything, but in every situation, by prayer and petition, with thanksgiving, present your requests to God. And the peace of God, which transcends all understanding, will guard your hearts and your minds in Christ Jesus."* - Philippians 4:6-7

Explanation: Philippians 4:6-7 offers a powerful antidote to anxiety: prayer. It encourages believers to bring their worries and concerns to God in prayer, with an attitude of thanksgiving and trust. The promise accompanying this instruction is profound: the peace of God, beyond human comprehension, will guard our hearts and minds in Christ Jesus. This peace is not dependent on our circumstances but on our relationship with God.

Biblical Examples: A poignant example of overcoming anxiety through reliance on God is seen in the life of the prophet Elijah (1 Kings 19). After a great victory over the prophets of Baal, Elijah faced intense fear and anxiety when threatened by Queen Jezebel. Fleeing into the wilderness, Elijah cried out to God in despair. In response, God met Elijah in his distress, providing him with sustenance, rest, and reassurance of His presence. Elijah found refuge in God's presence, demonstrating the power of prayer in overcoming anxiety.

In the New Testament, Jesus Himself exemplifies reliance on prayer during times of distress. In Mark 1:35, Jesus rises early in the morning to pray, seeking solitude and communion with His Father.

Similarly, in the Garden of Gethsemane, facing the prospect of His impending crucifixion, Jesus turns to prayer for strength and guidance (Luke 22:39-46). In both instances, Jesus finds solace and direction through prayer, modeling the importance of communing with God in times of anxiety.

Application: To overcome anxiety, we must actively replace anxious thoughts with prayer and trust in God's provision. Begin by identifying areas of anxiety in your life and bringing them before God in prayer. Pour out your heart to Him, expressing your concerns and fears, but also remembering to thank Him for His faithfulness and provision. As you surrender your worries to God, trust in His promises and rest in the assurance that His peace will guard your heart and mind. Cultivate a habit of regular prayer, seeking God's presence and guidance in every situation, and experience the transformative power of His peace in your life.

Day 8: Pursuing Purpose

Bible Verse: *"For I know the plans I have for you, declares the Lord, plans to prosper you and not to harm you, plans to give you hope and a future."* - Jeremiah 29:11

Explanation: Jeremiah 29:11 provides assurance that God has a specific plan and purpose for each individual. This verse assures believers that God's plans are not intended to harm but to prosper, giving hope and a future. It invites us to trust in God's guidance and provision as we seek to fulfill our purpose and calling in life.

Biblical Examples: One striking example of pursuing purpose in the Old Testament is seen in the life of Esther. When faced with the opportunity to intercede on behalf of her people, Esther recognizes her unique purpose and boldly steps into her role, despite the potential dangers (Esther 4:14). Through her courage and obedience, Esther fulfills God's purpose for her life, ultimately bringing about deliverance for the Jewish people.

In the New Testament, Jesus serves as the ultimate example of purposeful living. He declares His purpose in Mark 10:45, stating that He came not to be served but to serve and to give His life as a ransom for many. Throughout His ministry, Jesus sacrificially served others, fulfilling God's redemptive plan and demonstrating the selflessness and love inherent in living out one's purpose.

Application: To pursue purpose in our own lives, we must first seek God's guidance and direction through prayer and scripture study. Take time to reflect on your talents, passions, and experiences, seeking to discern how God may be calling you to use them for His glory. Embrace opportunities to serve others and make a difference in your sphere of influence, trusting that God will equip and empower you to fulfill His purpose for your life. Remember that purpose is not static but evolves as we grow in our relationship with God and respond obediently to His leading. Stay open to His direction, remaining flexible and willing to step out in faith as He unfolds His plans for you. As you pursue purpose with faithfulness and diligence, you will experience the fulfillment and satisfaction of living out God's intended destiny for your life.

Day 9: Finding Strength in Unity

Bible Verse: *"How good and pleasant it is when God's people live together in unity!"* - Psalm 133:1

Explanation: Psalm 133:1 celebrates the beauty and power of unity among God's people. It paints a picture of harmony and cooperation, highlighting the blessings that come from living in unity with one another. Unity is not merely the absence of conflict but the presence of genuine love, respect, and support among believers, reflecting the unity within the Godhead.

Biblical Examples: In the early days of the Christian church, unity among believers was a hallmark of their community. Acts 2:44-47 describes how the early Christians lived together in unity, sharing their possessions and supporting one another in times of need. This unity was a testament to the transformative power of the Holy Spirit and the deep bond shared by those who were part of the body of Christ.
Jesus Himself prayed for unity among His disciples in John 17:20-23, emphasizing the importance of love and unity in bearing witness to the world. He prayed that His followers would be one, just as He and the Father are one, demonstrating the inseparable bond and mutual love shared among believers.

Application: To apply this verse in our lives, we must actively seek opportunities to build unity within our communities of faith. This starts with cultivating an attitude of love, humility, and grace towards one another, recognizing and celebrating the diversity of gifts and perspectives among believers. Look for ways to foster cooperation and collaboration, working together towards common goals and missions. Embrace reconciliation and forgiveness, seeking to mend relationships and bridge divides where necessary. As we strive for unity in the body of Christ, we bear witness to the transformative power of God's love and bring glory to His name.

Day 10: Persevering Through Trials

Bible Verse: *"Consider it pure joy, my brothers and sisters, whenever you face trials of many kinds, because you know that the testing of your faith produces perseverance."* - James 1:2-3

Explanation: James 1:2-3 challenges believers to view trials not as obstacles to be avoided but as opportunities for growth and refinement. It encourages us to embrace trials with joy, knowing that they have the potential to strengthen our faith and produce perseverance, leading to spiritual maturity and steadfastness.

Biblical Examples: One of the most profound examples of perseverance through trials is seen in the life of Job. In Job 1-2, Job undergoes unimaginable suffering and loss, yet he remains faithful to God, declaring, "The Lord gave, and the Lord has taken away; blessed be the name of the Lord" (Job 1:21). Despite facing intense physical and emotional pain, Job perseveres in his faith, ultimately experiencing restoration and blessing from God (Job 42:10-17).

In the New Testament, Jesus Himself endured trials and temptations in the wilderness (Matthew 4:1-11). Faced with hunger, exhaustion, and the allure of worldly power, Jesus relied on God's Word and strength to overcome temptation, demonstrating the power of perseverance in the face of adversity.

Application: To persevere through trials, we must first adopt the right perspective, viewing trials as opportunities for growth rather than setbacks. Instead of allowing trials to discourage or defeat us, we can lean into God's presence and promises, trusting that He is with us and will sustain us through every trial. Cultivate a spirit of gratitude and joy, recognizing that God is at work in the midst of our struggles, shaping us into the image of Christ. Draw strength from the examples of perseverance found in Scripture, seeking to emulate their faith and resilience in your own life. And above all, continue to press on in faith, knowing that the testing of your faith produces perseverance, leading to a deeper intimacy with God and a steadfastness that withstands the storms of life.

Day 11: Living Generously

Bible Verse: *"Each of you should give what you have decided in your heart to give, not reluctantly or under compulsion, for God loves a cheerful giver."* - 2 Corinthians 9:7

Explanation: 2 Corinthians 9:7 emphasizes the importance of generosity and cheerful giving among believers. It encourages a heart attitude of willingness and joy in giving, rather than giving out of obligation or compulsion. This verse underscores the principle that giving is an act of worship and stewardship, acknowledging that all we have ultimately belongs to God.

Biblical Examples: One of the most poignant examples of generous giving is seen in the story of the widow's offering in Mark 12:41-44. Despite her poverty, the widow gave all she had—two small coins—as an offering to God. Jesus commended her sacrificial giving, highlighting the value of her gift in contrast to the larger but less sacrificial offerings of others. The widow's act of generosity serves as a powerful reminder that true giving is measured not by the amount but by the heart behind it.
Jesus Himself exemplified the importance of generosity and selflessness throughout His life and teachings. In Luke 6:38, He teaches, "Give, and it will be given to you. A good measure, pressed down, shaken together and running over, will be poured into your lap. For with the measure you use, it will be measured to you." Jesus also emphasized the significance of caring for the less fortunate in

Matthew 25:34-40, teaching that whatever we do for the least of His brothers and sisters, we do unto Him.

Application: To live generously, we must cultivate a heart of gratitude and stewardship, recognizing that all we have is a gift from God. Begin by prayerfully considering how you can give back to God and bless others with your time, talents, and resources. Be intentional in your giving, deciding in your heart what to give with joy and enthusiasm. Seek opportunities to support ministries, organizations, and individuals in need, both within your community and beyond. As you live generously, trust in God's provision and delight in the opportunity to partner with Him in furthering His kingdom on earth.

Day 12: Seeking Wisdom

Bible Verse: *"If any of you lacks wisdom, you should ask God, who gives generously to all without finding fault, and it will be given to you."* - James 1:5

Explanation: James 1:5 highlights the importance of seeking wisdom from God, who is the ultimate source of all wisdom and understanding. It assures believers that God is willing to bestow wisdom generously upon those who ask, without reproach or reservation. This verse underscores the value of wisdom in decision-making, discernment, and righteous living.

Biblical Examples: An exemplary demonstration of seeking wisdom is found in the story of Solomon's request for wisdom in 1 Kings 3:5-14. When offered anything he desired by God, Solomon humbly asked for wisdom to govern God's people with justice and discernment. Impressed by Solomon's request, God granted him not only wisdom but also wealth and honor. Solomon's example teaches us the importance of prioritizing wisdom above earthly treasures and seeking God's guidance in all aspects of life.

Jesus Himself serves as a model of wisdom and spiritual growth. In Luke 2:52, it is noted that Jesus grew in wisdom and stature, demonstrating the importance of continual learning and growth in wisdom throughout His life. Additionally, Jesus often retreated to solitary places to pray and seek guidance from His heavenly Father, showing the necessity of prayer in gaining wisdom and discernment.

Application: To seek wisdom, approach each day with a humble and teachable spirit, recognizing your need for God's guidance and understanding. Spend time in prayer, asking God to grant you wisdom in making decisions and navigating life's challenges. Delve into Scripture regularly, seeking wisdom and insight from God's Word. Be open to the counsel of wise mentors and fellow believers, recognizing that God often speaks through others to impart wisdom. As you prioritize seeking wisdom, trust in God's promise to generously bestow it upon you, knowing that He desires to guide you in paths of righteousness and understanding.

Day 13: Resting in God's Presence

Bible Verse: *"Come to me, all you who are weary and burdened, and I will give you rest."* - Matthew 11:28

Explanation: Matthew 11:28 extends an invitation from Jesus to find solace and renewal in His comforting presence, especially for those feeling burdened by the trials of life. This verse speaks to the innate human need for rest and reassurance, assuring us that true rest is available through Jesus. It emphasizes the restorative power of seeking refuge in His love and provision.

Biblical Examples*:* Throughout the Old Testament, we see examples of individuals finding rest in God's presence. One such instance is Elijah's retreat to Mount Horeb in 1 Kings 19, where he sought refuge and renewal after facing opposition and persecution. In the quiet solitude of the mountain, Elijah encountered God's comforting presence, finding strength to continue his mission.

Jesus Himself exemplified the importance of seeking solitude and communion with God. In Mark 1:35, we see Jesus rising early in the morning to pray, demonstrating the significance of carving out moments of stillness amidst busyness. By prioritizing His relationship with the Father, Jesus found rejuvenation and guidance for His ministry.

Application: To experience the rest promised by Jesus, we must intentionally create space in our lives for quietude and communion with God. This might involve setting aside dedicated time for prayer, meditation, or simply being present with God. As we lay down our burdens and worries before Him, we can find true rest and renewal in His loving presence.

Day 14: Embracing Change

Bible Verse: *"See, I am doing a new thing! Now it springs up; do you not perceive it? I am making a way in the wilderness and streams in the wasteland."* - Isaiah 43:19

Explanation: Isaiah 43:19 reassures us of God's sovereignty over change, emphasizing His ability to bring about new beginnings and opportunities even in the most challenging circumstances. Embracing change becomes an act of trust in God's plan and guidance.

Biblical Examples*:* The journey of the Israelites through the wilderness toward the Promised Land illustrates God's provision and leading during times of transition and change (Exodus 13-14). Despite their uncertainty, God made a way for them where there seemed to be none.
In the New Testament, we witness the transformative power of embracing change through the lives of Jesus' disciples. When Jesus called Peter, Andrew, James, and John to follow Him in Matthew 4:18-22, they left behind their familiar lives as fishermen to embark on a new journey with Jesus. Their willingness to embrace change led to profound transformation and the spread of the gospel.

Application: Embracing change requires faith and trust in God's faithfulness. Rather than resisting change out of fear or discomfort, we can surrender to God's plan, believing that He is making all things new. By maintaining an open heart and mind, we position ourselves to experience growth, transformation, and the fulfillment of God's purposes in our lives.

Day 15: Choosing Joy

Bible Verse: "*Rejoice in the Lord always. I will say it again: Rejoice!*" - Philippians 4:4

Explanation: Philippians 4:4 exhorts believers to rejoice in the Lord always, emphasizing the importance of cultivating a spirit of joy rooted in God's presence and promises. This verse challenges us to find our source of joy not in our circumstances, which are often fleeting and uncertain, but in the unchanging character of God and His faithfulness.

Biblical Examples: A powerful illustration of choosing joy amidst adversity is found in the story of Paul and Silas in Acts 16:25-34. Despite being unjustly beaten and thrown into prison, Paul and Silas choose to praise God and sing hymns in the darkness of their cell. Their act of worship not only demonstrates their unwavering faith and trust in God but also leads to a miraculous intervention, resulting in their freedom and the salvation of their jailer and his household. Paul and Silas' response to suffering serves as a powerful example of choosing joy regardless of circumstances.

Jesus Himself serves as the ultimate model of choosing joy in the face of suffering. Hebrews 12:2 tells us that Jesus endured the cross for the joy set before Him, focusing on the eternal perspective rather than the temporary pain and suffering of the crucifixion. His sacrificial love and obedience to the Father's will exemplify the profound joy that comes from living in alignment with God's purposes and promises.

Application: To apply Philippians 4:4 in our lives, we must practice choosing joy daily, regardless of our circumstances. This begins with intentionally shifting our focus from the challenges and hardships we may face to the goodness and faithfulness of God. Cultivate a spirit of gratitude by counting your blessings and acknowledging God's presence in your life. Seek out opportunities for worship and praise, even in the midst of trials, knowing that God is worthy of our praise at all times. As you choose joy in every circumstance, you will experience the transformative power of God's joy, which transcends the ups and downs of life.

Day 16: Navigating Relationships

Bible Verse: *"Above all, love each other deeply, because love covers over a multitude of sins."* - 1 Peter 4:8

Explanation: 1 Peter 4:8 underscores the paramount importance of love in all relationships. It exhorts believers to love one another deeply, emphasizing that love has the power to cover over a multitude of sins. This verse challenges us to prioritize love and compassion in our interactions with others, fostering unity, reconciliation, and mutual edification.

Biblical Examples: A beautiful illustration of selfless love and devotion is found in the story of Ruth and Naomi in the book of Ruth (Ruth 1-4). Despite facing loss and hardship, Ruth demonstrates unwavering loyalty and love for her mother-in-law Naomi, choosing to remain by her side and care for her needs. Ruth's sacrificial love ultimately leads to redemption and restoration for both her and Naomi, showcasing the transformative power of selfless devotion in relationships.

Jesus Himself exemplifies the highest standard of love in His commandment to His disciples in John 13:34-35: "A new command I give you: Love one another. As I have loved you, so you must love one another. By this everyone will know that you are my disciples if you love one another." Jesus' sacrificial love, demonstrated through His death on the cross, serves as the ultimate model of love for believers to emulate in their relationships with one another.

Application: To navigate relationships according to 1 Peter 4:8, prioritize love and compassion above all else. Extend grace and forgiveness to others, recognizing that love covers over a multitude of sins. Practice active listening and empathy, seeking to understand and empathize with the experiences and perspectives of those around you. Be intentional in your words and actions, choosing to build others up rather than tearing them down. Above all, seek unity and harmony in your relationships, allowing the transformative power of love to mend brokenness and bring healing and reconciliation. As you prioritize love in your relationships, you will reflect the character of Christ and bear witness to His love to the world around you.

Day 17: Walking in Humility

Bible Verse: *"Do nothing out of selfish ambition or vain conceit. Rather, in humility value others above yourselves."* - Philippians 2:3

Explanation: Philippians 2:3 calls believers to embody humility in their interactions with others, admonishing against selfish ambition and vain conceit. Instead, it urges them to esteem others above themselves, reflecting the selfless and servant-hearted attitude modeled by Christ. Humility is not merely a lack of pride or self-importance but an active posture of placing the needs and interests of others before our own.

Biblical Examples: One of the most profound demonstrations of humility is witnessed in the account of Jesus washing His disciples' feet in John 13:1-17. Despite being the Son of God and their Lord, Jesus takes on the role of a servant, stooping to wash the feet of His disciples—a task typically reserved for the lowest servant. In doing so, Jesus not only models humility but also teaches His disciples the importance of serving one another with love and humility.

Jesus Himself serves as the ultimate model of humility. Philippians 2:5-8 describes how Jesus, though equal with God, humbled Himself by taking on human form and willingly submitting to death on the cross for the redemption of humanity. His sacrificial act exemplifies the depth of humility and love that believers are called to emulate in their lives.

Application: To walk in humility according to Philippians 2:3, intentionally cultivate a mindset of humility in your daily interactions. Consider the needs and interests of others before your own, seeking opportunities to serve and uplift those around you. Practice active listening and empathy, valuing the perspectives and experiences of others. Be willing to admit your own faults and shortcomings, embracing a posture of continual growth and learning. By imitating Christ's example of humility, you not only reflect His character to the world but also contribute to the building of genuine and harmonious relationships within the body of Christ.

Day 18: Restoring Hope

Bible Verse: *"For I know the plans I have for you, declares the Lord, plans to prosper you and not to harm you, plans to give you hope and a future."* - Jeremiah 29:11

Explanation: Jeremiah 29:11 offers a message of hope and assurance from God to His people. It declares God's intimate knowledge of His plans for His children, plans characterized by prosperity, protection, and a hopeful future. This verse reminds believers that God's plans are ultimately for their welfare and not for harm, instilling confidence and trust in His sovereign purposes.

Biblical Examples: The context of Jeremiah 29:11 is set during the Babylonian exile, a period of immense suffering and despair for the Israelites. Despite their circumstances, God reassures them of His faithfulness and redemptive plans for their future. The subsequent verses (Jeremiah 29:10-14) depict God's promise to restore His people from exile, demonstrating His unfailing love and commitment to their restoration and renewal.

Jesus' resurrection from the dead serves as the ultimate source of hope for believers. In 1 Corinthians 15:20-22, Paul declares that Christ's resurrection ensures victory over sin and death, offering the promise of eternal life to all who believe in Him. Through His resurrection, Jesus provides the ultimate assurance of hope—a hope that transcends earthly trials and points to the glorious future awaiting believers in eternity.

Application: To restore hope according to Jeremiah 29:11, anchor your trust in God's unchanging character and promises. Seek solace and assurance in His word, meditating on the truth of His faithfulness and provision. When faced with challenges and uncertainties, cling to the hope found in Christ's resurrection, knowing that He has conquered sin and death once and for all. Cultivate a spirit of confident expectation, trusting that God's plans for your life are good and purposeful. As you rest in the hope of God's promises, you will find strength and perseverance to endure trials and embrace the future with joyful anticipation.

Day 19: Embracing Authenticity

Bible Verse: *"Therefore, if anyone is in Christ, the new creation has come: The old has gone, the new is here!"* - 2 Corinthians 5:17

Explanation: 2 Corinthians 5:17 proclaims the transformative power of being in Christ. It declares that when someone becomes a follower of Jesus, they are fundamentally changed—old ways of thinking and living are replaced by new life in Him. This verse calls believers to embrace their identity in Christ fully and authentically, free from the constraints of pretense and insecurity.

Biblical Examples: The story of Zacchaeus in Luke 19:1-10 provides a powerful example of authenticity and transformation. Zacchaeus, a tax collector despised by society, encounters Jesus and is profoundly changed by the encounter. He publicly repents of his dishonest practices and commits to making restitution to those he has wronged. Zacchaeus' genuine transformation demonstrates the radical impact of encountering Jesus and embracing new life in Him.

Jesus Himself serves as the ultimate model of authenticity. Throughout His ministry, Jesus welcomed and accepted people from all walks of life, inviting them to come to Him as they were. In Matthew 9:9-13, Jesus calls Matthew, a tax collector, to follow Him, demonstrating His willingness to embrace even those considered outcasts by society. Jesus' unconditional acceptance and love for people exemplify the authenticity and grace that characterize life in Him.

Application: To embrace authenticity according to 2 Corinthians 5:17, begin by fully accepting and embracing your identity in Christ. Recognize that in Him, you are a new creation, free from the bondage of your past and empowered to live authentically for Him. Allow God to work in and through you, embracing your uniqueness and sharing your story with transparency and vulnerability. Be honest about your struggles and shortcomings, trusting in God's grace to cover your weaknesses. As you live authentically in Christ, you will experience the freedom and joy that come from living in alignment with His truth.

Day 20: Cultivating Inner Peace

Bible Verse: *"Peace I leave with you; my peace I give you. I do not give to you as the world gives. Do not let your hearts be troubled and do not be afraid."* - John 14:27

Explanation: John 14:27 offers a profound promise of peace from Jesus Himself. He assures His disciples that He is leaving them with His peace—a peace that transcends worldly circumstances and understanding. This peace is not fleeting or conditional but rooted in the unchanging character of God and His presence with His people.

Biblical Examples: The account of Jesus calming the stormy sea in Mark 4:35-41 illustrates His authority over chaos and His ability to bring peace in the midst of turmoil. As the disciples faced a violent storm that threatened to capsize their boat, Jesus spoke a word of rebuke to the wind and waves, instantly calming the sea. His miraculous act not only revealed His divine power but also demonstrated His desire for His disciples to experience His peace in the midst of life's storms.
Jesus Himself serves as the ultimate model of inner peace. Despite facing trials, persecution, and ultimately death on the cross, Jesus remained steadfast and at peace, rooted in His trust in God's sovereignty and His eternal purposes. In John 16:33, Jesus assures His disciples that in Him, they can have peace even in the midst of tribulation, knowing that He has overcome the world.

Application: To cultivate inner peace according to John 14:27, surrender your worries and anxieties to God in prayer, trusting in His provision and care for you. Practice mindfulness and meditation on Scripture to center yourself in God's peace, allowing His presence to calm your restless heart. Cultivate a spirit of gratitude and thanksgiving, focusing on the blessings and goodness of God in your life. Guard your heart and mind against fear and anxiety, choosing instead to fix your thoughts on God's promises and faithfulness. As you abide in Christ and His peace, you will experience a deep and abiding sense of tranquility that transcends the chaos of the world around you.

Day 21: Encountering God's Grace

Bible Verse: *"But because of his great love for us, God, who is rich in mercy, made us alive with Christ even when we were dead in transgressions—it is by grace you have been saved."* - Ephesians 2:4-5

Explanation: Ephesians 2:4-5 beautifully articulates the essence of God's grace. It speaks of God's boundless love and mercy toward humanity, despite our sinful state. Through His grace, God offers forgiveness, redemption, and new life through Jesus Christ. This verse highlights that salvation is a gift from God, undeserved and unmerited, given freely out of His abundant love and mercy.

Biblical Examples: The parable of the prodigal son in Luke 15:11-32 vividly illustrates the concept of God's grace. Despite squandering his inheritance and living a life of rebellion, the prodigal son is welcomed back with open arms by his father, who lavishes him with love, forgiveness, and acceptance. This parable demonstrates the unconditional nature of God's grace, which is freely extended to all who repent and turn back to Him.

Jesus Himself exemplifies God's grace in His encounter with the woman caught in adultery in John 8:1-11. Rather than condemning her according to the law, Jesus extends grace and mercy, inviting her to go and sin no more. This interaction showcases Jesus' compassion and forgiveness, emphasizing His desire for repentance and transformation rather than judgment.

Application: To fully experience God's grace according to Ephesians 2:4-5, begin by acknowledging your need for His forgiveness and salvation. Embrace His grace with gratitude and humility, recognizing that it is a gift freely given through faith in Jesus Christ. Allow God's grace to transform your heart and life, leading you to live in obedience and service to Him. Furthermore, extend the same grace you have received to others, showing generosity, compassion, and forgiveness to those around you. As you encounter God's grace and extend it to others, you will experience the fullness of His love and redemption in your life.

Day 22: Cultivating Resilience

Bible Verse: *"Consider it pure joy, my brothers and sisters, whenever you face trials of many kinds, because you know that the testing of your faith produces perseverance."* - James 1:2-3

Explanation: James 1:2-3 challenges believers to adopt a counterintuitive perspective toward trials and tribulations. Instead of viewing them solely as sources of pain and suffering, James encourages believers to consider them as opportunities for growth and character development. Trials, when approached with the right attitude, can strengthen faith, build resilience, and deepen dependence on God.

Biblical Examples: The apostle Paul serves as a powerful example of resilience in the face of adversity. Despite enduring countless hardships, including beatings, imprisonment, and persecution, Paul remained steadfast in his faith and commitment to Christ. In 2 Corinthians 11:23-28, Paul provides a glimpse into the various trials he faced for the sake of the Gospel, yet he persevered with unwavering resolve and trust in God's faithfulness.

Jesus Himself exemplifies resilience through His endurance of the cross. Hebrews 12:1-3 urges believers to fix their eyes on Jesus, who endured the shame and suffering of the cross for the joy set before Him. Jesus' willingness to endure suffering and death, motivated by His love for humanity and obedience to the Father's will, serves as a model of resilience and steadfast faith.

Application: To cultivate resilience according to James 1:2-3, adopt a mindset of joy and perseverance in the midst of trials. Instead of allowing difficulties to discourage or defeat you, view them as opportunities for spiritual growth and refinement. Lean into God's presence and promises during difficult times, trusting that He will provide the strength and endurance needed to overcome. Seek support and encouragement from fellow believers, fostering a sense of community and solidarity in navigating life's challenges. As you persevere through trials with faith and resilience, you will experience God's transformative work in your life and witness the beauty of His faithfulness in every circumstance.

Day 23: Embracing God's Provision & Supply

Bible Verse: *"And my God will meet all your needs according to the riches of his glory in Christ Jesus."* - Philippians 4:19

Explanation: Philippians 4:19 assures believers of God's faithfulness to provide for their every need. It emphasizes that God's provision is not limited by earthly resources but is rooted in His boundless riches and glory. This verse invites believers to trust in God's unwavering faithfulness and to rely on Him for both spiritual and material provisions.

Biblical Examples: The story of Elijah and the widow of Zarephath in 1 Kings 17:8-16 illustrates God's miraculous provision during a time of famine. Despite the scarcity of food, God commands Elijah to stay with a widow in Zarephath, promising that her flour and oil will not run out until the end of the famine. Through this miraculous provision, God demonstrates His sovereignty over the natural elements and His faithfulness to sustain His people in times of need.

Jesus Himself serves as the ultimate example of God's provision through His feeding of the five thousand in Matthew 14:13-21. When faced with the challenge of feeding a large crowd with limited resources, Jesus multiplies five loaves of bread and two fish to provide more than enough food for everyone present. This miraculous provision highlights God's abundant generosity and His ability to meet the needs of His people beyond their expectations.

Application: To embrace God's provision according to Philippians 4:19, cultivate gratitude and contentment in every circumstance, trusting in God's faithfulness to provide. Recognize that God's provision extends beyond physical needs to include spiritual sustenance, such as His grace, wisdom, and peace. Practice stewardship and wise management of resources, acknowledging that everything we have ultimately comes from God. Rely on God's provision with confidence and faith, knowing that He is faithful to meet our needs according to His riches and glory.

Day 24: Seeking God's Guidance

Bible Verse: *"Trust in the Lord with all your heart and lean not on your own understanding; in all your ways submit to him, and he will make your paths straight."* - Proverbs 3:5-6

Explanation: Proverbs 3:5-6 offers timeless wisdom on seeking God's guidance in all aspects of life. It encourages believers to trust in God wholeheartedly, surrendering their own limited understanding and plans to His infinite wisdom and sovereignty. By submitting to God's will and direction, believers can experience the assurance that He will lead them on the straight and righteous path.

Biblical Examples: The Israelites' journey through the wilderness, guided by the pillar of cloud and fire, exemplifies God's guidance and provision for His people. In Exodus 13:21-22, God leads the Israelites out of Egypt and through the wilderness by manifesting His presence as a pillar of cloud by day and a pillar of fire by night. This divine guidance reassures the Israelites of God's faithfulness to lead them to the Promised Land and protect them along the way.
Jesus' life and ministry also serve as a model of seeking God's guidance. In Matthew 26:39, Jesus prays in the Garden of Gethsemane, submitting His will to the Father's plan, even unto death on the cross. Despite knowing the suffering that awaited Him, Jesus obediently surrenders to God's will, demonstrating the importance of prayerful dependence on God's guidance in decision-making.

Application: To seek God's guidance according to Proverbs 3:5-6, cultivate a lifestyle of prayer and surrender to God's will. Trust in His wisdom and sovereignty, even when His plans may differ from your own. Seek counsel from godly mentors and community members, recognizing the value of seeking wisdom from others. Be attentive to God's leading through Scripture, prayer, circumstances, and the counsel of the Holy Spirit. Surrender your desires and plans to God's perfect will, trusting that He will direct your steps and lead you on the path of righteousness and blessing.

Day 25: Celebrating God's Faithfulness

Bible Verse: *"The Lord is faithful to all his promises and loving toward all he has made."* - Psalm 145:13b

Explanation: Psalm 145:13b highlights the unwavering faithfulness of God to His promises and His love for all His creation. It encourages believers to celebrate and acknowledge God's faithfulness as an essential aspect of His character. This verse serves as a reminder that God's faithfulness extends to every aspect of life, providing assurance and hope in His steadfast love and care.

Biblical Examples: An exemplary demonstration of celebrating God's faithfulness is found in the Israelites' observance of festivals and feasts commemorating God's deliverance from slavery in Egypt. In Exodus 12:14, God instructs the Israelites to celebrate the Passover as a perpetual memorial of their redemption from bondage. Through these festivals, the Israelites recalled and celebrated God's faithfulness in fulfilling His promises and delivering them from oppression.

Jesus serves as the ultimate model of faithfulness in fulfilling God's promises. In Matthew 5:17, Jesus declares that He has come not to abolish the Law or the Prophets but to fulfill them completely. Throughout His earthly ministry, Jesus demonstrated unwavering faithfulness to God's mission, fulfilling every prophecy and promise of God with precision and perfection.

Application: To apply Psalm 145:13b in daily life, take time to reflect on God's faithfulness in your own life journey. Recall moments when God has proven Himself faithful and loving toward you, despite challenges or uncertainties. Express gratitude and praise for His steadfast love and provision. Cultivate a habit of celebrating God's faithfulness through worship, prayer, and thanksgiving. Share testimonies of God's faithfulness with others to encourage and uplift them in their faith journey.

Day 26: Building Resilient Faith

Bible Verse: *"So do not fear, for I am with you; do not be dismayed, for I am your God. I will strengthen you and help you; I will uphold you with my righteous right hand."* - Isaiah 41:10

Explanation: Isaiah 41:10 offers profound assurance and comfort to believers, reminding them of God's constant presence, strength, and assistance. It encourages individuals to anchor their faith in God's promises rather than succumb to fear or dismay. This verse serves as a foundational truth for building resilient faith in God's unwavering care and protection.

Biblical Examples: The story of Daniel exemplifies resilient faith in the face of adversity. Despite facing persecution and threats, Daniel remained steadfast in his devotion to God and continued to trust in His protection and deliverance. In Daniel 6, Daniel's commitment to prayer leads to his miraculous deliverance from the lion's den, demonstrating the power of unwavering faith in God's promises.
Jesus' teachings also emphasize the importance of trusting in God's care and provision. In Matthew 6:25-34, Jesus encourages His disciples not to worry about their basic needs but to trust in God's provision, just as He cares for the birds of the air and the flowers of the field. Jesus assures His followers that God will strengthen and uphold them with His righteous hand.

Application: To build resilient faith according to Isaiah 41:10, anchor your trust in God's promises and His presence. Combat fear and discouragement with the assurance of God's constant companionship and assistance. Nurture your faith through regular prayer, meditation on Scripture, and fellowship with other believers. Lean on God's strength and seek His guidance in times of uncertainty or difficulty. Trust that God will uphold you with His righteous hand and provide everything you need to navigate life's challenges with confidence and resilience.

Day 27: Embracing God's Love

Bible Verse: *"For God so loved the world that he gave his one and only Son, that whoever believes in him shall not perish but have eternal life."* - John 3:16

Explanation: John 3:16 encapsulates the profound depth of God's love for humanity. It declares that God's love is not passive but sacrificial, demonstrated through the gift of His Son, Jesus Christ. This verse underscores the universality and transformative power of God's love, offering eternal life to all who believe in Him. It serves as a foundational truth for believers to embrace and embody God's boundless love in their lives.

Biblical Examples: A poignant example of someone encountering God's unconditional love is found in the story of the Samaritan woman at the well (John 4:1-42). Despite her past and societal stigma, Jesus extends compassion, acceptance, and forgiveness to her, revealing the depth of God's love that transcends cultural barriers and prejudices. Through this encounter, the Samaritan woman experiences a profound transformation and becomes a witness to God's love in her community.

Jesus stands as the ultimate model of sacrificial love. Romans 5:8 emphasizes that God demonstrates His love for humanity through Jesus' death on the cross, even while humanity was still in rebellion against Him. Jesus willingly laid down His life to reconcile humanity to God, manifesting the highest expression of divine love through His selfless sacrifice.

Application: To apply John 3:16 in daily life, embrace the depth and breadth of God's love for you personally. Allow His love to penetrate every aspect of your being, transforming your thoughts, attitudes, and actions. Cultivate a heart of gratitude for the sacrificial love demonstrated through Christ's death and resurrection. Extend God's love to others by demonstrating kindness, compassion, and forgiveness. Live as a reflection of God's love, drawing others into relationship with Him through your words and deeds.

Day 28: Pursuing Holiness

Bible Verse: *"But just as he who called you is holy, so be holy in all you do; for it is written: 'Be holy, because I am holy.'"* - 1 Peter 1:15-16

Explanation: 1 Peter 1:15-16 exhorts believers to pursue holiness in every aspect of their lives, mirroring the character and nature of God. Holiness encompasses purity of heart, integrity, and obedience to God's commands. It is a reflection of God's own holiness and righteousness, calling believers to live set apart from the patterns of this world and to walk in accordance with His will.

Biblical Examples: Joseph's story in Genesis 39 provides a compelling example of someone who pursued holiness amidst temptation and adversity. Despite facing pressure to compromise his integrity, Joseph remains steadfast in his commitment to honor God. His refusal to yield to Potiphar's wife's advances demonstrates his dedication to living a life of holiness and righteousness, even in the face of great temptation.
Jesus serves as the ultimate model of holiness. In His earthly ministry, Jesus exemplified perfect obedience to God's will and lived a life of moral purity. He calls His disciples to follow Him in holiness, teaching them to strive for perfection as their heavenly Father is perfect (Matthew 5:48). Through His sacrificial death and resurrection, Jesus empowers believers to pursue holiness through the indwelling presence of the Holy Spirit.

Application: To pursue holiness according to 1 Peter 1:15-16, commit yourself to a life of obedience to God's Word and His commands. Guard your heart and mind against sinful influences and temptations, seeking purity in your thoughts, words, and actions. Cultivate intimacy with God through prayer, study of Scripture, and fellowship with other believers. Surrender your desires and ambitions to God's will, allowing His Spirit to transform you from the inside out. Strive for holiness not out of legalism but out of a genuine desire to honor God and reflect His character to the world.

Day 29: Trusting in God's Guidance

Bible Verse: *"Trust in the Lord with all your heart and lean not on your own understanding; in all your ways submit to him, and he will make your paths straight."* - Proverbs 3:5-6

Explanation: Proverbs 3:5-6 advises believers to trust in the Lord wholeheartedly and rely on His wisdom rather than their own understanding. This verse encourages surrendering one's plans and decisions to God, acknowledging His sovereignty and guidance in every aspect of life. By submitting to God's will and seeking His direction, believers can experience the assurance that God will lead them on the right path.

Biblical Examples: The Israelites' journey through the wilderness provides a profound example of trusting in God's guidance. As they followed the pillar of cloud by day and the pillar of fire by night, they relied on God's direction to lead them to the Promised Land, demonstrating the importance of trusting God's guidance even when the way forward seems uncertain (Exodus 13:21-22).
Jesus' reliance on His Father's guidance is evident throughout His earthly ministry. In John 5:19, Jesus declares that He does nothing on His own but only what He sees the Father doing, highlighting His complete submission to God's will and guidance. This reliance on God's guidance ultimately led Jesus to fulfill His mission of redemption through His death and resurrection.

Application: Believers can cultivate trust in God's guidance by seeking His will through prayer, studying His Word, and listening for His voice. Surrendering one's plans and decisions to God and being open to His leading can bring clarity and direction in life's decisions. Trusting in God's guidance also involves patience and willingness to wait for His timing, trusting that He will make our paths straight as we submit to Him in all things.

Day 30: Walking in Wisdom

Bible Verse: "*The fear of the Lord is the beginning of wisdom, and knowledge of the Holy One is understanding.*" - Proverbs 9:10

Explanation: Proverbs 9:10 teaches that true wisdom begins with a reverent fear of the Lord and a deep knowledge of His character. This verse emphasizes the importance of aligning our thoughts and actions with God's truth, leading to a life characterized by discernment, righteousness, and understanding. Walking in wisdom involves seeking God's guidance and applying His principles to every aspect of our lives.

Biblical Examples: King Solomon, known for his wisdom, demonstrated his wisdom when he was presented with a difficult case of two women claiming to be the mother of a child (1 Kings 3:16-28). Solomon's wisdom in this situation, where he proposed to divide the child to satisfy both women, revealed his discernment and understanding of human nature.

In Luke 2:41-52, the young Jesus astounded the teachers in the temple with His wisdom and understanding of the Scriptures. Despite His age, Jesus displayed a deep knowledge of God's word and an ability to apply it to His life.

Application: Believers can walk in wisdom by seeking God's guidance through prayer and studying His word. Applying biblical principles to decision-making, seeking counsel from wise mentors, and living a life that honors God can help believers grow in wisdom. Additionally, cultivating humility and a teachable spirit allows God to impart His wisdom and understanding to those who seek it.

Day 31: Living with Hope

Bible Verse: *"May the God of hope fill you with all joy and peace as you trust in him, so that you may overflow with hope by the power of the Holy Spirit."* - Romans 15:13

Explanation: In Romans 15:13, the Apostle Paul prays for believers to experience the fullness of hope, joy, and peace that come from trusting in the God of hope. This verse emphasizes the foundational role of hope in the Christian life, highlighting its transformative power to bring joy and peace even amidst life's uncertainties and challenges. Living with hope involves placing our trust in God's promises and provision, knowing that He is faithful to fulfill His word and guide us through every circumstance.

Biblical Examples: The Apostle Peter's letter to the believers encourages them to set their hope fully on the grace to be revealed when Christ returns (1 Peter 1:13). Despite facing persecution and trials, Peter urges believers to maintain steadfast hope in the promise of Christ's return and the inheritance awaiting them in heaven. By anchoring their hope in the future grace to be revealed, believers can endure present sufferings with patience and confidence in God's faithfulness.
Jesus as the Model: Jesus' resurrection from the dead serves as the ultimate demonstration of hope for believers. Through His victory over sin and death, Jesus offers the assurance of eternal life and the promise of redemption to all who believe in Him (1

Corinthians 15:20-22). Jesus' resurrection not only validates His divinity but also serves as the foundation of Christian hope, providing the assurance of forgiveness, reconciliation with God, and the hope of a future glorified existence.

Application:

1. Anchor your hope in God's promises: Spend time studying and meditating on God's Word to familiarize yourself with His promises. Reflect on passages that speak of His faithfulness, provision, and plans for your future.
2. Cultivate trust through prayer: Develop a habit of prayer, bringing your hopes, dreams, and concerns before God. Trust in His sovereignty and goodness, knowing that He hears your prayers and is working all things together for your good.
3. Maintain a positive perspective: Choose to focus on the blessings and victories in your life rather than dwelling on setbacks or disappointments. Cultivate an attitude of gratitude and praise, recognizing God's faithfulness in every season.
4. Support and encourage others: Share your hope and faith with others who may be struggling or in need of encouragement. Offer words of comfort, support, and prayer, pointing them towards the hope found in Christ.
5. Live with anticipation: Embrace each day with confidence and anticipation of the future God has prepared for you. Trust that His plans are

for your welfare and not for harm, to give you a future and a hope (Jeremiah 29:11).

Conclusion

As we come to the end of **'My Daily Cup of Energizer: *Finding Strength, Joy, and Purpose Each Day through HIS Word'***, may you carry with you the timeless truths and practical wisdom gleaned from its pages. Throughout this journey, we've explored the depths of God's love, the power of faith, the importance of gratitude, and the significance of hope. Each day, as you sipped your coffee and delved into the Scriptures, may you have found renewed strength, encouragement, and inspiration for your daily walk with God.

Remember, the Christian life is not about perfection but about progress. It's about daily seeking God's presence, trusting in His promises, and living out the principles of love, forgiveness, and grace. As you face the challenges and joys of each day, may you continue to grow in your relationship with God, deepening your faith and reflecting His light to the world around you.
But this is not the end; rather, it's just the beginning of a lifelong journey of faith and transformation. Let this book serve as a guidepost, a reminder of the truths you've encountered, and a source of encouragement in times of need. And as you close its pages, may you go forth with renewed vigor, ready to embrace each day with hope, joy, and a heart overflowing with gratitude.

May the God of all grace continue to fill you with His Spirit, strengthen you with His power, and lead you in His ways. And may your life be a living testimony to

His love and faithfulness, shining brightly in a world that so desperately needs the light of Christ.

Thank you for embarking on this journey with me. May God bless you abundantly as you continue to walk in His truth and experience the fullness of His blessings in your life.

Amen.

About the Author 'GERARD ASSEY'

Gerard Assey is a Graduate in Economics, a PGD in Management (HRD) and holds a Doctorate in Leadership. Gerard holds several International Qualifications in Sales, Debt Collection, Training & Teaching, and is a 'Fellow' of the prestigious 'Institute of Sales & Marketing Management'-UK, a Certified NLP Practitioner, a 'Certified Trainer', an 'Accredited Management Teacher-Behavioral Sciences', a 'Certified Competency Facilitator', a 'Certified Management Consultant'- (the International credentials of a professional management consultant, awarded in accordance with global standards of the ICMCI); and a Certification from the University of Michigan in 'Successful Negotiation: Essential Strategies and Skills'

He is also a Member of the 'National Association of Sales Professionals' backed with several years experience in varied industries, both in India and Overseas. He also holds an 'Etiquette Consultant' Certification from the USA (by Sue Fox, Author of Best Seller: 'Business Etiquette for Dummies'. She has trained some of the top celebrities' world over). He was also a recipient of a scholarship for extensive training in Japan on 'Corporate Management for India'.

Gerard Assey is 'Founder & Chief Corporate Trainer' of the Group: '**Citius, Altius, Fortius Unlimited'**- an organization that **celebrated 20 years of Glorious Service** in 2021, focusing on 3 Core Competencies:

People. Performance. Profit; in functional areas of Sales & Marketing, HR & Organizational Development, covering Recruitment, Training & Consultancy!

Having managed organizations with large Sales Forces in India & Overseas, his specialization cover extensive areas of Sales Training (All levels - Presentation, Negotiation, Key/ Strategic Accounts Management & Managerial Skills for all sectors), Bid Proposal/ Capture Planning/ Management Trainings, Retail Sales, Customer Service & Customer Retention Programs, Training for Prevention & Collection of Debt, Self & Personal Development Programs (Time Management, Teamwork & Team Building, Business Etiquette & Personal Grooming, Leadership & Managerial Skills, People Management Skills, Train-the-Trainer etc), including preparation of Custom-designed Business Manuals for Internal (HR, Induction, and Sales etc) & External use (Instruction, User Manuals).

Gerard has successfully conducted over 6100 Trainings & Workshops (as of Mar '24) all across India, Middle East, Africa, Europe & S.E. Asia. Besides public programs conducted regularly, both in India & Overseas, he has some of the top names as clients whom he services from Single Owners to large Public & Government undertakings, covering all sectors, for their in-house needs.

His website: www.CollectionSkills.com is the only one in this part of the world to be featured in the 'Collections & Credit Risk Magazine-USA' under 'Who's Who in Training' and ranks TOP, along with other websites listed below on most search engines.

Gerard is author of 118 books already (April 2024),

A few of our business related books:

1. Bite-sized Bits on Commonsense Management
2. Heart to Heart on Life's Principles'
3. How to become a Successful Manager
4. The Sales Professionals' Master Workbook of S.Y.S.T.E.M.S
5. The Professional Business Email Etiquette Handbook & Guide
6. The Professional Business Video-Conferencing Etiquette Handbook & Guide
7. Professional Presentation Skills
8. Exceptional Customer Service
9. Professional Tele-Marketing Skills
10. Professional Debt Collection Skills
11. The G.R.E.A.T. Sales & Service Workbook
12. Sales Training Advantage for Results (*The Ultimate Sales Training Manual to enable you stand out as a S.T.A.R.*)
13. CEO Daily Planner & Organizer
14. The Sales Professionals' Master Daily Planner
15. The Professional Debt Collector's Master Daily Planner
16. My Daily Planner & Organizer
17. MY EMERGENCY INFORMATION RECORD (Family Emergency & Peace of Mind Planner)
18. The Ultimate Therapist & Counselors Planner and Organizer
19. Building an Ethical Workplace
20. Managing Relationships at Work
21. Managing Business Meetings Effectively
22. Effective Delegation Skills
23. Goal Setting for Success
24. B2B Selling by Email
25. Professional Business Etiquette & Grooming
26. Dining Etiquette & Table Manners
27. Effective Networking Skills
28. Grooming, Etiquette & Manners for Teens, Young Adults & Future Leaders
29. Inter-Personal Skills
30. Get Ready, Get Hired!
31. Selling in a Recession
32. Effective Receivables Management in an Economic Downturn!
33. Real Estate & Property Sales Training

34. Credit Sales & Accounts Receivable Management
35. Selling Skills for Real Estate & Property Advisors
36. Take G.R.E.A.T. C.A.R.E!
37. Spa, Salon & Health Club Selling Skills
38. Selling Travel, Holiday & MICE Services
39. Selling Skills for Spa's, Salons & Health Clubs
40. Retailing in Salons & Spas
41. Selling Holiday, Vacation, Tours & Packages
42. The Power of Sales Referrals
43. Selling Luxury
44. Technical Selling Skills
45. Financial Advisors Sales Training
46. Dealing with Burnout at Work Monopolize Your Markets
47. Selling to Affluent Customers
48. Growing up with Grace
49. Financial Selling Skills
50. *The Effective Manager's Guide: Key Skills to Thrive*
51. From Aspiring to Inspiring: A Guide for New Managers on the Rise
52. The Power of Focus
53. Selling with Integrity: Sell Like Jesus The Perfect Role Model!
54. 31 Habits of Champions: Your 31-Day Journey to Greatness
55. Rejecting Grasshopper Talk: From Grasshopper to Giant-Killer-*Defeating Giants Daily!*
56. Navigate the AI-Powered Future of Bid & Proposals: Up-Skill to Stay Relevant with Alternative Career Paths & Opportunities
57. Hiring Sales Winners
58. Present with Impact
59. Success Unlocked: *Breaking Free from Habits that Hold You Back*
60. Complaints to Cheers, Feedback to Gold: Mastering Complaints Management
61. Thriving Together: *Cultivating Diversity, Equity, and Inclusion*
62. Coaching Skills for Sales Managers
63. Soaring to Success in Business & Leadership: Swifter, Higher, Stronger!
64. From Classroom to Podium: A Student's Guide to Powerful Public Speaking & Presentation Skills

65. Developing Self-Discipline
66. The CEO's 31-Day Power Plan: Unlocking Success through Essential Traits
67. Credibility Matters
68. A Winning Attitude
69. Bid & Proposal Management Using AI
70. Sales Forecasting: A Practical & Proven Guide to Strategic Sales Forecasting
71. Elevate & Energize: *50 Dynamic & Fun Activities for Peak Workplace Morale*
72. 'Sales SOS! Sales on Fire! *30 Days to Conquer Chaos & the Nightmares of Success!'*
73. Mastering Sales Managerial Skills: *Building High-Performing Teams & Driving Exceptional Results*
74. Eagle-Eyed Leadership: Unleashing the Power of 31 Lessons from Eagles
75. The Ultimate Employee Training Guide: *Training Today, Leading Tomorrow*
76. Being More Accountable at Work
77. Creating a Culture of Continuous Improvement
78. Effective Questioning & Listening Skills
79. The Power of Value Selling
80. The Growth Mindset
81. Mastering Professional Help Desk Skills
82. The Power to Lead with Empathy
83. Being Prepared: The Key to Unlocking Success

From the Ministry side, Gerard graduated in the very first batch of Charis Bible College-India & had for over 9 years served as a Part-time Faculty at Charis Bible College-Chennai (Andrew Wommack Ministries-Colorado, USA).
He is also a graduate of the Advanced Mentorship Program (AMP) and the Circle Of Ministerial Engagement (C.O.M.E.) of Prophet Jerome Fernando and a Spiritual Son of the Esteemed Prophet.
An accomplished author of several Secular & Christian Books, Gerard has been on the board of a few international organizations and boasts of being the SON

of the MOST HIGH GOD: An ordinary guy following an extraordinary GOD!

...And some of his most recent Christian Books being:

1. A Bouquet of Praises for My KING
2. Christian Jokes for the Serious Religious' Folks!
3. Jesus Healed You!
4. Praise24Ever! (also in Tamil version)
5. The 5G Network of GOD
6. Building Faith over F.E.A.R- FACE EVERYTHING AND RISE with JESUS
7. Hebrew and Greek Praise and Worship Words
8. Godly Mothers' and Grandmothers' Bible Story time for Kids!
9. Miracles of Jesus in Pictures
10. Raise your Praise all 365 Days
11. Thanking GOD with an Attitude of Gratitude
12. Meditating on the Attributes of GOD
13. Puppet Scripts
14. Alcohol Ruins, JESUS Reforms, Renews & Restores!
15. Habakkuk 2:2 Christian Daily Journal, Planner & Organizer
16. ABC of GOD's Word for Handwriting Practice
17. Daily Bible Verse Handwriting Practice (Building Godly Character & Faith through Cursive Handwriting Practice!)
18. Guiding Light: Fun & Faith-Building Bible Activities for Children
19. Rejecting Grasshopper Talk: From Grasshopper to Giant-Killer-*Defeating Giants Daily!*
20. Teen Titans of Faith: *Building Courage, Determination & Christ-like-Esteem*
21. I AM Empowered: *Unleashing Divine Power with Positive Declarations*
22. Be A Solution Provider-*From Passion to Purpose*: *A Biblical Guide to Being the Answer to the World!*
23. Miracles of JESUS
24. Parables of Jesus for a Meaningful Life!
25. A Grateful Heart: Importance of Sharing Testimonies of GOD's Grace
26. Melodies of Worship to JESUS: 31 Songs of Praise & Worship From My Heart to HIS!
27. I AM SO BLESSED!
28. My Daily Cup of Energizer

Besides regularly contributing to business & trade journals, including international ones such as the 'Creative Training Techniques' and the 'Sales News' of the U.S.A, He is also a member of several prestigious bodies & trade associations, having participated in many Conferences & Workshops in India & Overseas.

Prior to his last assignment of leading & managing a large MNC as head, Gerard had a 3-year stint in the Middle East as a Consultant with a leading British Consultancy Firm.

As the past 'Official Country Representative' for the International Business Award- 'THE STEVIES'-(the business world's own Oscar) for about 4 years- he ensured a few Indian companies that qualify for the same every year!

Gerard can be contacted at:
Email: training@Sales-Training.in,training@CollectionSkills.com
Websites:

www.Sales-Training.in
www.EtiquetteWorks.in
www.CollectionSkills.com
www.RetailSalesTraining.in
www.SalesTrainingIndia.com
www.ManualPreparation.com
www.TrainingWithPuppets.com
www.FirstContactAcademy.com
www.SalesAndMarketingRecruiter.com

Our TRAININGS that can help your team

- ✓ **Sales Effectiveness**: Selling Skills for any Sector: Service/ Logistics/ FMCG Realty/ Insurance & Finance/ Media/ SPA's, Health Clubs & Salons/ Key Account Management, Effective Negotiation Skills/ Bid & Proposal Management Skills/ Retail Sales Training: Any Sector (Auto, Jewelry, Clothing, Luxury etc)
- ✓ **Customer Service Skills**-Complaints Handling & Customer Retention
- ✓ **Debt Prevention & Collection Skills**
- ✓ **Etiquette & Grooming**
- ✓ **Leadership & Managerial Skills**
- ✓ **Self & Personal Development Skills**: Presentation Skills/ Effective Communication Skills/Business Proposal Writing Skills/ Problem Solving & Decision Making Skills/ Empowering Secretaries-The perfect PA! (For Secretaries & PA's)/ Effective Time Management/ Teamwork & Teambuilding/ P.R.I.D.E- **P**ersonal **R**esponsibility **I**n **D**elivering **E**xcellence

www.ingramcontent.com/pod-product-compliance
Lightning Source LLC
LaVergne TN
LVHW010119170826
845678LV00012B/2488

* 9 7 8 8 1 9 7 1 1 2 1 2 6 *